Artifacts of Desire and Loss

Cynthia Hernandez

Copyright © 2016 Cynthia Hernandez
All rights reserved.
ISBN-10:1532714513
ISBN-13:9781532714511

Just a few words beautifully strung together...

Acknowledgements and Dedication

This collection of poems has been a long time in creation. It would not have come together without the encouragement and support of these people who always made me feel like my words were worth sharing: Heather Chamberlain (my creative advisor, personal champion and therapist); Kelli Williams (my closest friend); Darcy McInnis (my love, my wife, and my life partner for the last 26 years); and Marcy Hernandez-Clark (my sister with a poet's heart and my first fan). I appreciate the love and support of all of my siblings, my parents and from Facebook friends and family who appreciate my Poetry Month posts, as well as a Tumblr following for my poems and photos. I consider myself an empathic poet, in that I draw inspiration for many of my poems from the experiences of others. I've written many poems inspired by friends and family. As those closest to me know, I feel things deeply and I value emotional connection with others. Often through this connection, I am left with a lot of feelings to process, and writing is the way I do that. Because I have a busy work and home life, I often turn to poetry and rhyme as my chosen format, because I like the focus required to express feelings in rhyme and the short format matches the short bursts of time I have.

The poems in this collection cover the breadth of human experiences, from the lilt of desire to the grip of heartache from the uncertainties of romance to the cavern of loss. The poems range from tongue-in-cheek to reverential. I hope you will find something in this collection that resonates with or delights you.

I welcome your feedback by review on Amazon.com. I also encourage you to follow me on Tumblr at cynderh.tumblr.com or to visit my Facebook page at:
http://facebook.com/PalomaCreates

In closing, I want to dedicate this book to my poet friend and mentor, Judith Kleck Powell, who was an example to me through her life, and through the grace she showed as she was dying. Judith was my first creative writing teacher while I was a college student at Central Washington University. For many years I aspired to write like Judith, but I eventually found comfort with expressing my own voice, and now in sharing it with you. Thanks for reading!

In the Name of the Muse

I write out my pain
in concise poems that rhyme.
Over and over
and time after time.

As if picking a scab
or cutting to feel,
through my poems and my words
my heartache is revealed.

But do I shy away?
No, I lean in hard.
I exploit my own pain
for the sake of the bard.

I mine my own suffering
for stuff I can use.
I embrace all that hurt
through the grace of the muse.

There Is Too Much Mystery

There is too much mystery in our every day.
When will I see you?
What will you say?
Does your heart feel pulled towards mine?
Will our wants and words align?

When we go to say goodnight
will you hold my hand or hug me tight?

Do you know I dream of you
and wish for things we shouldn't do?

And when at last you rest your head,
do you want me in your bed?

Tomorrow is another day.
When will I see you?
What will you say?

The Question

Is it yes?
Or is it no?
Are you planning to stay?
or preparing to go?

My ears heard you whisper
that you'd always be near.
But my heart feels so hollow,
and my head's filled with fear.

I want you to stay,
but I want what is true.
So if you really don't feel me,
then it's best that we're through.

Please be honest and tell me
what I need most to know.
Is it a yes?
Or is it a no?

Undone

I am a shadow
        In love with the sun.

She enters the room
and I come undone.

There's something like magic
        In her eyes and her smile.
Her charms, they ensnare me,
        her flirtations beguile.

Where we are headed
        neither is sure.
But my heart's love of hers
        is constant and pure.

My perspective is altered.
        My nature is changed.
My life as I've known it
has been rearranged.

I am a shadow
        In love with the sun.

In the heart of my heart,
I know she's the one.

Texting

Thinking of you on this beautiful day
and all of the things I wanted to say
and all of the things you'll never know
about the ways I love you so.
Instead I send a smiley face
and hope that you read in its place
all those words stored up in me
that I'm so afraid to let you see.

One day, who knows what fate might bring
I may open up, and you'll hear me sing
of feelings deep and love so true
that it would just astonish you.

But here instead it's still today
and I just wrote
with this to say: ☺

Spring

Today
while walking
a gentle breeze
tapped me
on the shoulder
and whispered
your name
in my ear.

Raindrops
like
wet memories
fell
leaving reflections of you
all around me.

Tomorrow
there's
sunshine
in the forecast.

You're coming
home.

Reunion

Is there
really such a thing as time,
when walking down 4th street today
I saw you

and my heart leapt up
to join with yours
in a dance backwards
across the decade

separating
your hands

from mine?

Reassurances

My love is ample.

Question it not.

My fears are wild.

Do not heed them.

My lips are
hot and full
with wanting.

Press yours to them
like a cool cloth
against a child's forehead.

My delight is evident.

I cannot disguise it.

These words are empty.

But my heart is full.

Pluviophile

I never cared
too much
for rain
but now I hear its
sweet refrain
and cannot help
but think of you.

In rain you find
a certain bliss
A soothing sound.
A liquid kiss.

A washing clean.
A start anew.
I hear rainfall
and think of you.

A Kiss In the Rain

Liquid grey feelings fall
And I, empty handed and wordless
seek cover and attempt to shrug away
the approaching cold
and the wandering desire
that threatens to consume me.

In the space between us,
you say, "this way."
I turn toward your command
and into your arms.
Your lips claim mine
behind the shield
of an umbrella you have raised.

A safe haven.
A secret place.
A moment in time.

Parting

You pull away
a band-aid
too soon
removed
from the wound.

You leave
pieces
of me
stuck
all over
you.

Bird in the Hand

A bird in the hand
is a good thing to keep,
but the two in the bush
keep invading my sleep.

In my dreams I keep chasing
their colors allure.
But when I awaken,
I need to feel sure.

So with the bird in my hand,
I feather our nest,
and convince my desires
that safety is best.

Adrift

A tiny boat
adrift at sea...
a beautiful uncertainty.

Where will these waters carry me?

Night Sky

In the lonely hours
before sleep's embrace
I search the night sky
for a wishing star.

In the silence of dark
I hold the wish in my mouth
like a seed of a dream
that in daylight
will take root.

Hindered

Your absence
has hindered my day.
I can't keep this longing at bay.
I search every crowd
for your eyes.
I utter your name in my sighs.

I pray that you'll come back to me.
I can't live without you you see.

It was wrong that I pushed you away,
when I was desperately
hoping you'd stay.

If I could have
just one more chance--
a fresh start to our broken romance...

there's nothing
that I wouldn't do
to get back
to the love we once knew.

Elevator Music

In the space between floors
I move toward you.
My fingers brush yours
as if by accident.

A spark of light and warmth
travels up my arm
and out my lonely mouth.

When we reach our destination
my arms encircle you
your arms encircle me
and we rest a moment from
the dance
and sway
to elevator music.

Yearning

Love, if you touch me
my yearning heart will unfold
like a rose in bloom.

Its petals will fall
and scatter color
around the places you walk.

Waves

It's the sounds
that touch me first.

They whisper words
 of love
 outside my range of hearing,
 tickling my ears with delight and
echoing a resonance I can feel.

Finding a new medium of expression
 they move over me
 wet, slow, insistent.

Their urgency wears at my substance
slowly, sweetly,
I surrender completely.

Myself now liquid,
I wash up on your shore.

Undoing

If you bask in my love
like a cat in the sun,
I'll show you so many
hot ways to have fun.

As our bodies entwine,
I'll be yours.
You'll be mine.

And together we'll
both come

undone.

Wordless

It starts with the slightest brushing of hands,
then fingers twine together with urgency.
I lift your hand to my lips and rest a kiss
first on the smooth of your knuckle,
then against the salt and sweet
of your palm.

In the wordless poetry of touch
 we are joined
in a moment
both fleeting
and eternal.

Seduction Reduction

Search my eyes

      and find my lips.

Reduce me

      to my lust.

On Entering Your Room
While You Were Away

Fingers of sunlight
        draw me
into your room, and
though I know you are not,
        I see you there—
cross-legged, eyes closed,
lips humming quietly
like you were in my dream:
the one where I am the sunlight
        kissing your sweet face,
the cool shadow reaching
        toward and
                away from you,
the pillow in the corner,
        crumpled and begging,
and the bed beneath you,

and the bed

beneath you,

and the bed

beneath

you.

My Little Death

The me that was me can no longer be;
when I am with you, you're all that I see.
I don't really mind this.
I've wanted to find this.

So go on,
feel free
to execute me.

If you kill me with kindness.
I'll die in your arms.
A smile on my lips.
In love with your charms.

I'll happily give up the me that was me.
If instead I can have you + me = we.

So go on,
feel free
to execute me.

Azul

Your eyes soothe me

like the cool blue of a lake

on a scorching hot day.

Mirage

Desert sands stretch out before me
as far as I can see.
My soul feels parched and dusty
because you're not here with me.

I'm going through the motions
not sure what else to do.
When suddenly before me
I see a glint of blue.

My heart lilts at the sight of this.
From my lips escapes a sigh.
The cool blue pool before me
is the exact color of your eyes.

Maya

All night in sleep
I saw your face
bold against the moonlit sky
smiling sweetly
smiling long.

The warm glow
of your gaze
weighed heavy
on my eyelids
on my yearning mouth.

Unwelcome morning
       shattered
sleep sublime.

Nap in the Sun

Nap in the sun
I dream of the one
who's not here with me
and
 never
      will
        be.

Longing: A triptych in Haiku

Longing:
Though my fingers ache
for the softness of your cheek,
I fold them away.

Longing II:
Though my lips yearn
to press warmth against your neck,
they whisper your name.

Longing III:
My heart beat quickens
at the nearness of you,
but I step away.

Libra

She handles the book
      like a lover
gently easing
      between the pages,
kissing,
    smelling,
        memorizing,
           everything.

Too long her fingers
      linger on its spine
caressing,
    coaxing,
        teasing,
           delighting.
The words leap from the page
      to kiss her
           back.

(for Darcy)

Let's Be Clear

I won't giggle and blush
like a girl with a crush
when you walk in the room.

But if what you desire
is a sensual fire
I'm the woman for you.

Free Me

Hither and yon I wandered free
not sure what I would find or see.
I looked for you over the years,
but all I found were endless tears.

Still, I kept moving, heart in hand--
hoping in time I'd understand.
why it was you went away--
why I couldn't make you stay.

Now the clock is ticking fast,
and I fear the time I have won't last.
If you have any love left for me,
won't you set my caged heart free?

First Kiss

After yearning too long
our lips crash together
tongues glide like dance
desperate to express emotions
failed by words.

Your eyes lock with mine
offering and begging
tenderness.

 My hands acquiesce –
an attempt to make you feel
the love coursing through my veins.

You touch me
and free the birds of longing
that too long have been caged.

Don't Promise Me Forever

Don't promise me forever,
when you don't know what it means.
Such lips as yours were meant for more
than shattering my dreams.

Just lie here now and kiss me.
This moment's all I need.
A promise is your word.
But I prefer the deed.

Forever sounds so lovely.
A whisper in my ear.
But it's just a fleeting fancy.
This cannot last I fear.

So hold me like you'll lose me,
like the clocks could stop tonight.
If there never was forever
At least we'd have one night.

Do Over

In that pause
as we were parting
I felt dormant fires restarting.

Confronted with your lips so near
I almost overcame my fear.

I want that moment
back again.

The next time
I will let love in.

Desire

Is it lust or desire?
I do not care.
I just want your fingers in my hair...

the feel of your breath
against my ear...
skin against skin
as you draw me near.

I wish for your hand
and mine entwined.
Please kiss me before
I lose my mind.

Communion

Because I can remember
 a time when
I knew not the leisure of
touching you
I touch slowly,
relish in each texture,
savor every smoothness.

Because I can imagine
a time when
I may lose the leisure of
touching you
I cling
to your body
like the passing moments
we call
life.

Confusion

Is this pleasure
or pain?

My heart isn't sure.

But my hands are busy
seeking answers.

And my
lips are
quite certain
they know.

Breathless

You leave me
breathless
whenever I'm with you.

When you're
in close proximity
there's little
I can do.

My hands begin to tremble;
they long to reach for you.
My mouth goes dry and dusty
afraid to leak the truth.

I focus on my breathing
and listen with intent.
But no matter how I try,
my craving won't relent.

As I rise to take my leave,
my knees begin to shake.
I try to play it cool,
but I feel a growing ache.

If I don't share this secret soon,
I believe I might expire.
If I can't express my love for you,
I'll be consumed by this desire.

A Plea

Respect my heart,
but let it stop there.

Deprave my body,
dishevel my hair.

Reduce me to my
basest desire.

Ignite the spark
from smolder to fire.

Immerse me
in your passions deep.

Then rock me into
blissful sleep.

A Simple Request

Your lips on mine
a kiss sublime
intoxicating
as fine wine.

I think about
this all the time.
I hope someday
you will be mine.

Until then don't deny me this:
let's please hold hands
if we can't kiss.

Wants and Needs

I never wanted less than this-
Your lips on mine,
an endless kiss.

Your hand in mine
to have and hold.
A love to last
until we're old.

There's nothing that I need so much
as your sweet smile,
your steady touch.
To know you're ever by my side.
My truest self I needn't hide.

I never wanted more than this-
your life and mine
in boundless bliss.

Wishful Thinking

I want for a freedom that is not mine:
your arms around me
closing the distance
between here
and tomorrow.

Your lips pressed against my own;
a punctuation mark ending our feeble utterings.

Your hand nested in mine;
a reassurance,
a warmth,
a tether
holding my heart to yours.

I want for a freedom that is not mine.

The Loneliest Night

I would gladly suffer
the loneliest night
if today I could have you
by my side.

I know you cannot
be mine to keep
but my love for you
runs true and deep.

If I had just one day
of you and me
I would relish it
for all eternity.

Even knowing the pain I'll feel
when you're gone,
I'd rather feel your love once
before we move on.

I would gladly suffer
the loneliest night.
If today I could have you
by my side.

Song Worm

Today I'm that song
that you don't want to hear.

The one that repeats
on a loop in your ear.

Incessant, insistent,
invading your brain...

endless repetition
that drives you insane.

And much like that vexing,
unstoppable song,

if you'd just surrender,
then I will move on.

Reckless Words

If I tell you your eyes to me are the sea,
will you see only charm
and not see the real me?

If I tell you your smile to me is the sun,
will that make you draw nearer,
or will that make you run?

If I tell you I want you to kiss and to hold,
will you think me brave-hearted,
or overly bold?

If I tell you I love you-
and want something more,
will you hold your arms open,
or show me the door?

On the Ride Home

My spoken name rests on your lips:

the kiss you held at bay.

Change of Heart

If I can't be your number 1,
then you can't have your spot of sun.
That's one thing I can take from you.
And I won't be your number 2.

If you don't have a change of heart,
my pride and I may have to part;
I'd rather be your number 2,
than face a day when there's no you.

Ellipses

It's the things
        you do not say
that press a hollow question mark
        against my heart
leaving me
        with nothing
to do
but wait.

False Hope

The winds of change
blow cool and soft
their whispers set my hope aloft.

I'm ready now
for something new
I wonder if you're ready too.

Seasons change.
Days pass by.
Closer still grow you and I.

Around the bend
of place and time,
I know someday
you will be mine.

Flavor of the Month

I never wanted to be
the flavor of the month.

But between that
and never having had your
soul touch mine

I'll take it.

I'm Not the One

I'm not the one you think about
when you fantasize.
I'm not the one whose name is in
the exhale of your sighs.
I'm not the one your heart desires
to hold within its keep.
I'm not the one you dream about
when in your slumbers deep.
I'm not the one you'll walk with
through all of your tomorrows.
I'm not the one you'll cling to
when life delivers sorrows.
I'm not the one who'll hold you
in your final days.
I'm just the one who loves you
in oh so many ways.

Neither Here Nor There

The fact that I adore you

 is neither here nor there.

Because while I am here,

in love with you,

you are

there.

If You Change Your Mind

And if you ever
change your mind
look for me
and you will find
that I will still be waiting here
unending love...

my soul laid bare.

Like Any Other Day

Today I want what I can't have
like any other day.
I know you want those same things too
no matter what you say.

Your casual air and easy charm
I hold now in contempt.
The grip you have upon my heart
will simply not relent.

I wish I'd find a way to be
as happy as you are,
content with what we know could be
but isn't in the stars.

If I might here appeal to you
to give yourself to me,
and if in turn you opened up
and set your feelings free,

I know we'd both lead richer lives
less sorrow and regret.
Your life and mine, our hearts entwined
a love we won't forget.

The End

Submit to me or walk away
this game is getting old.
I've wanted you to be with me,
but you won't be so bold.

I've tried to play by rules you set
while showing you my heart,
Now I'm filled with deep regret,
and feel it's best we part.

I've lost so much pursuing you.
And I'd do it all again.
You won't show me that you love me too.
So it seems we've reached the end.

Unburden Me

The words that I refuse to say
abrade my heart most every day.
It hurts to hold my tongue this way.

But if I free these words inside
and see my hopes and fears collide
I wonder will my heart survive?

Unlock my heart—you hold the key
So won't you please unburden me?
And say the words to set me free?

A Proposal

There's so much more
I need in life
than to wear a white dress
and be somebody's wife.

I want a great love,
like most people do,
but I don't need
something old,
something borrowed, or blue.

I'd rather lie here beside you,
gazing into your eyes,
exchanging deep truths
and not marital lies.

Let's not promise a lifetime
of love and devotion.
Let's just relish this current
delicious emotion.

If we do this well,
one sweet day at a time.
I'll always be yours,
and you'll always be mine.

Open Doors

A ring is not the only thing
that can bind my heart to yours.
I don't need vows and promises.
My love needs open doors.

I know the ring is just the thing
that we are taught to crave.
As if it holds some power
to keep a love enslaved.

But I want a love that's free
to breathe the open air,
where every day we choose
the next day to be there.

I'd rather know I'm wanted
than feel something's owed to me.
I'd rather feel love daily
and yet know we both are free.

Perfection Is Overrated

The perfect couple
we will never be,
but that doesn't really matter to me.
I value authenticity.

And perfection is overrated.

So show me your raw,
and I'll give you my real.
Together we'll get through
whatever we feel.

Love can be messy.
It can hurt like hell.
But a life without love
is a life not lived well.

Love Is Blind

I guess I've always known the score.

You love with one foot out the door.

I knew you were the leaving kind.

But I loved you,

and love is blind.

The Will & The Way

You once loved me I know,
now you're breaking my heart.
If you can't finish this shit,
then why did we start?

I recited your name
like it was my own.
Now I'm left looking lost
and feeling alone.

The passion between us
you just couldn't trust.
I said it was love,
but you thought it was lust.

I'm not sure what to say,
or where this will go,
and no matter what else,
there's one thing I know:

You loved me before
and I love you still.

I'll find the way,
if you find the will.

Stay

The novelty of me
has worn away.
And now it seems
you want to stray.

I knew that this
was your M.O.
So many people
told me so.

Now I'm not one to
force your hand,
but if I could make
you understand...

my love for you
was not for play.
I had hoped it would last.
I had hoped you would
                              stay.

Soul Kiss

If I could kiss your soul,
then you would know
I love you deeper
than flesh and bone.

But in this realm
of lip and tongue,
something's been lost
in translation.

Shadowlight

By the light of your love
my shadow was born.
All my wrongs you made right
with the sweet of your warm.

Then as day fell to night
and my love turned to fear,
I both wanted you gone,
and I wanted you near.

You're my heart and my hurt
my pleasure and pain.
My umbrella for shelter
and a cold frigid rain.

And as truth clears the lies,
my once blind heart sees—
what I hoped was forever,
now never will be.

One Day

In the afterglow
we seemed to know
we'd left our love
nowhere to go.

So I walked away,
while you pleaded "stay,"
but there was really
nothing more to say.

I think of you
from time to time.
I wonder how you are.

If I only knew
where to find you,
I'd soothe and kiss
this scar.

Falconry

You had me trained to return on cue.
So you let me fly away from you.

I spread my wings and lifted off.
I soared so high, my landings soft.

Until one day I flew so high,
I knew if I returned
I'd die.

So with just one
backward glance,
or two
I flew
and flew
away from you.

I left you there, an outstretched arm.
I didn't mean you any harm.

I only knew I had to fly.
That if I returned
I just might die.

Ilunga*

*A person who forgives the first transgression, tolerates the second, but never a third.

I was born with a forgiving heart.
I knew you'd test it from the start.
You hurt me when you said goodbye.
Then you returned for "one more try."
I took you back with open arms.
I was so persuaded by your charms.
But you betrayed me once again.
It seems in love I'll never win.

So desperately I wanted you,
I saw past transgression number two...
believed you when you said you'd changed,
and let my life be rearranged.

But now you've hurt me one last time.
I couldn't forgive you if I tried.
You've had your chances--more than one.
I've had enough. Get out! I'm done.

Stalemate

You won't let me leave,
but I don't want to stay.
I'm so ready to end
this false love we portray.

But I can't break your heart,
and you won't let me go,
so we just carry on--
hope our falsehood won't show.

There's no move to be made.
It seems we are stuck
in this endless stalemate.
And I'm bitter as fuck.

Mouthful of Regret

It seemed we had it all,
but was it just pretend?
We once had everything,
and now we're scarcely friends.

We took so much for granted,
and forgot we had to try.
We're both left empty handed,
and there's little wonder why.

Love isn't always easy,
but it needn't be this hard.
It's for the best that we should part now,
before we're both left deeply scarred.

Nothing Left To Say

I don't need black roses
to tell me that we're through.
Though I've tried denying it,
I see now that it's true.

Don't pretend you give a damn.
I see it in your eyes.
I'd rather face the ugly truth,
than hear more of your sweet lies.

I held out hope for far too long,
that we could salvage this.
It's clear we need to move along,
but let's first seal it with a kiss.

Because if all I get to take from this,
are memories of what we once had.
I'll take a few more as we part
to dwell on when I'm sad.

I wish you every happiness
as you travel on life's way.
I loved you once, you loved me too.
There's nothing left to say.

Beautiful Ruins

Our love burned like
a field ablaze--
left us both standing in a haze
of flamed out passions
and broken words.
We were left grounded
like wingless birds.

We hobbled along
across barren lands.
Our damaged hearts were in our hands.
And in this apocalyptic state
we had to learn to accept our fate.

What once had been
could no longer be.
All that was left of you and me
was a beautiful ruins
for as far
as the eye
could see.

Aftermath

The morning after we parted ways
My head was in a mournful haze.
My heart felt heavy in my chest.
I wondered if what we'd done was best.

I cried until I had no tears.
I visited my darkest fears.
I held your pillow close to me.
And wished for my soul to be set free.

I'm Sorry

I'd ask for absolution,
but it isn't yours to give.
Instead I'll have to suffer
with the awful things I did.

I know I didn't mean them—
that I acted out in hurt.
But that doesn't make it better.
It only makes it worse.

Courageous Hearts

Quietly I walked away,
though all I wanted was to stay.
I found myself unable to speak.
In my vulnerability I was weak.

Just as you were turning toward me,
I turned away, afraid to see
that your love for me
matched mine for you;
in a world so false,
we'd found something true.

But this much goodness
I had never known.
And in finding it,
my heart was thrown.
I didn't know what to do or feel.
I'd never felt something so real.

I hope to one day start anew—
stake a claim for me and you.
With courageous hearts
we'll rise above
our persistent fears
to embrace our love.

Becoming Schadenfreude

I never wanted to be this way--
to find pleasure in someone else's dismay.
But life's disappointments have ravaged me,
and now I'm someone I never wanted to be.

My mouth is full of bitterness.
My mind is dark with anguished twists.
The charity that I once knew
left long ago, along with you.

I have asked for love to rescue me,
but all around, it's loss I see.
So with empty heart, I forge ahead,
becoming Schadenfreude instead.

Cave Dwellers

Empty handed and wordless
I showed up at your door.
Nothing could prepare me
for the depths we would explore.

You told me you like caves
and find comfort in the dark.
But in your eyes there danced a light,
and in that light I found a spark.

My fears caught in my throat,
and my heart was in your hands.
My emotions were failed by words,
and yet you seemed to understand.

The Key

Before there was a you and me,
my heart and mind were far from free.
I'd locked my precious treasures there,
and no one knew or seemed to care.

Constrained was I by loss and pain,
so much to lose, not much to gain.
And there I stayed all locked away,
forgetting until that magic day.

Meeting you was like a spark--
igniting light, dispelling dark.
You welcomed me with open arms,
there I took shelter, safe from harm.

Then something took ahold of me.
With open eyes I began to see...
brighter colors, richer sounds,
inspiration all around...

a sense of freedom,
bold and new.
The whole of me
embraced by you.

You've been my muse,
restored my dreams,
when I'm with you
my spirit beams.

My heart soars
like a bird aloft.
My roughest edges
now made soft.

I cannot thank you adequately
I just hope you know
what you've done for me.
You, dear friend have been my key.

(for Kelli)

The Keeper

With shoulders broad
and open arms,
you keep so many
safe from harm.

Insightful words.
A giving heart.
A gentle nudge
toward a new start.

You help transform
so many lives.
In light you shed
fresh hope arrives.

Within your care
and guiding touch
I hope you know
I've healed so much.

In my gratitude and love
toward you
I hope you find
some healing too.

(for Heather)

Tree of Creativity

The fruits that fell
when you shook my tree
each revealed a part of me...
things that I had never shared
in poems and words my soul was bared.

And in time these outgrowths
of my heart
my life revealed,
a work of art.

(for HLC)

The Creator

On the bleak blank canvas
fog of morning

I imagined beauty
and color
Into existence.

And in that
I found my power.

The Fixer

I've been broken many times before.
Found myself face down on the cold hard floor.
And each time I got up again,
determined not to let loss win.

But this time was a brutal blow.
Life's cruel twists had hurt me so.
I floundered on that wretched floor,
not sure I could get up once more.

A bitter uncertainty kept me there.
I didn't feel. I didn't care.
My sense of hope abandoned me.
The darkness made it hard to see.

I wished someone would lend a hand,
or care enough to understand.
But they all passed busily on their ways.
While I stayed on that cruel floor for days.

Then through my brokenness a light emerged.
Some dormant strength within me surged.
Like a plant that reaches toward the light,
I found hope to live and a will to fight.

So I gathered my pieces and rose above.
Replaced self-loathing with self-love.
Opened my eyes to finally see
the one that I needed to fix me was me.

Health Scare

Your news today
brought me to tears-
evoking all my wildest fears.

I cannot bear imagining
you feeling ill or suffering.

But you are strong
and stubborn too
and life holds much
in store for you.

So don't despair
or think the worst.
It's best to just
put first things first.

Stay positive.
Go through the tests.
And just keep hoping
for the best.

I'm here for you.
Always will be.
Don't hesitate
to call on me.

And through it all
I wish you grace
and the comfort of
love's warm embrace.

Take heart, my friend.
Have courage too.
This illness is
no match for you.

Poem for a Scary Day

When all seems lost, and you don't know which
way the road will bend,
reach out your hand and find mine here:
my heart, my sleeve, your friend.

And if your life delivers you
a burden or a scare,
then let me carry half the load,
you'll always find me there.

I wish I had "one liquid word"
to make you worry less.
But just like you, I'm frightened too.
I'm shaken, I confess.

For you to me, my dearest friend,
are something like the sun.
Those spots of gray you chase away,
with mirth and wit and fun.

I couldn't bear for you to face life's troubles on
your own.
So I am here to tell you dear,
you'll never walk alone.

Faith Beyond the Clouds

When storm clouds gather
and darken your sky
when life's circumstances
leave you wondering why
when the future's uncertain
and the path is unclear
just reach out to me
        and you'll find me right here.

Hang on to your faith
and hold tight to belief
that love beyond words
can dispel any grief.

Always in My Dreams

An insistent rain
pelts the roof
calling me back
from sleep.

At morning's edge
I rise
and grasp
at dream images
I want to keep.

Most of these escape me,
elusive thoughts it seems.
But then I see you smiling...
you are always in my dreams.

Garden Tender

I walked past your garden,
in the fading light of day
and saw there all the flowers
that return to bloom each May.

Lobelia, Aster, Bluebells,
Forsythia and Foxglove
all bloom in sweet remembrance
that you planted them with love.

Though you've been gone for many years,
your garden thrives here still.
Forget-me-nots remind us
that we never will.

Comes the Dawn

The dawn delivers a reckoning
that restless sleep denied.
Awake, deep sorrow stirs my soul
that you're not by my side.

I set my feet on the cold floor
and stand to face the day.
I'm not sure how to carry on
since you have gone away.

Jayme

It is not on rainy days
        that I miss you most,
but on fragrant spring mornings that
cling,
glistening,
to each delicate blade of grass in the pasture.

If I close my eyes to inhale the fragrance,
        the sun blazes a painting of you:
trotting through the pasture,

thirteen,

you turn the Arabian in my direction
and wave.

I move toward the fence to meet you,
the details of your face unexpectedly vivid:

Even the sun cannot match the gold of
your hair spinning into one intricate braid.

Closer,
the freckles on your face sparkle
        like miniature constellations.

(In loving memory of Jayme Arvidson)

Loss

A fragrant night, a cloudless sky
A dream I had off you and I.

When I awoke you weren't around.
My heart cried out without a sound.

No pretty night or sunny day
can take my sense of loss away.

Memory Road

The sky is filled with sadness
as the leaves begin to fall.
In their final days their colors blaze
--an ending none can stall.

The car window frames a picture
of memories spanning years.
My heartache overtakes me
the image blurred by tears.

The road stretches on before me.
I drive on along my way.
Though the past beckons to me
I can visit, but mustn't stay.

Funeral Songs
A Triptych in Haiku

Cemetery Rain
Rain beats a rhythm
against your burial home.
Hollowness engulfs.

Twenty-One Guns
3 guns fire 7 shots;
each one a cry for more time.
Rain and tears become one.

Poll Bearers
Six in black suits
carry you home;
laying rosebuds
in farewell.

(In loving memory of Rhonda Sue Desmarais)

Twilight

In the space between

here
        and
                gone

    you linger.

I wonder

    if words

        or wishes

matter there...

or if they float by

like clouds

on the horizon

    between

        remembering

and forgetting.

Walk On - *(for Judith Kleck)*

Barren tree...
clear blue sky....
glistening waters catch my eye.
Though you're not here,
I feel you still.

A poet's heart,
A fighter's will.
Your words endure,
a piece of you,
now part of me,
you've been set free.

As I walk on,
I know you're near ...
your voice a whisper in my ear.

I see so much to put to words...
tongue-wagging dogs,
elusive birds...
the smiles on faces passing by,
I feel a tear escape my eye.

Although you're here
you're also gone.
I miss you so.
But I'll walk on.

What Night Brings

Like a blanket of temporary forgetting,
night falls.

In the realm of sleep and dreams
all is possible and impossible at once:

A delicious fiction.
A release of fears.
A place of connection between
what is, what was, and
what can never be.

Morning arrives, like a rooster's call.

Realities impose.

What night served up as poetry,
the dawn rewrites as prose.